Intermedia
For

By Andrew Howell

Table of Contents

Introduction

If you think about it, it rather makes sense that no one seems to know where the first playing cards came from. Some say that cards are hundreds of years old, and they were first used in China.

Others say that King Charles VI of France had his painter make a deck of special cards for him!

Many agree that playing cards started as what we now call Tarot cards. Tarot cards, like the ones pictured above, are kind of modern card decks because they also have numbered and trump cards. That is where the same-game ends, though. Tarot cards use pictures instead of symbols and their suits are Cups, Wands, Swords and Pentacles. In addition, as well as the regular deck, Tarot cards also have a series of cards with different pictures on them. Fortune-tellers use these cards to predict the future and reveal mysteries.

What is interesting is that even though playing cards may have originally come from Tarot cards hundreds of years ago, both of these types of cards are still being used.

No matter how they first came about, card decks used to cost a lot of money before printing presses were invented. Only the richest people had enough money to buy them.

Could you imagine paying thousands of dollars for a plain old pack of cards?

The very first ones were round. About 500 years ago, they started to be made rectangular, with pictures of kings and queens on them.

Having a deck of playing cards was even against the law at one point!

Today, they definitely are not against the law, and a pack costs only a few dollars. Almost everybody has owned a deck or two in their life, or maybe played a game of cards with friends.

So where does card magic come from?

Like the invention of playing cards, no one is sure how cards worked their way into magic acts. Tricks were probably being used long before magicians ever started using them in their acts. In the 1800's, Joseph Pinetti, because he was such a smooth talker, became the very first entertainer to be allowed to show off his card magic tricks in an actual theatre... and the audience loved it!

His success was so huge that card magic started to become kind of a big deal.

In modern times, it was the magician Howard Thurston who became the first person to be considered a master card manipulator. Many of the tricks he invented are still done today, by magicians like David Copperfield and David Blaine...and many more.

All those master magicians make card magic look so easy, don't they?

It is not until you try card magic yourself that you realise the tricks are not all as easy as they look. The tricks you will find here certainly are not that easy.

In fact, they were picked **because** they are challenging.

That is okay, though. You are a smart cookie, and you are here because you want to learn some card tricks that are a little harder, right?

So read on.

Learn some new things.

Have some fun.

As Many as You

How You Do It:

1. Pick someone from your audience. Let us call him Jack.
2. Get Jack to take a few cards off the top of the deck, without showing you which cards he has or how many.
3. Next, you take a few cards. Make sure you take more than Jack does, <u>but do not let him see that you have taken more</u>.
4. Ask Jack to turn around and count his cards in his head.
5. Count your own cards at the same time.
6. It does not matter how many cards you really have, but let us pretend you have 17 cards.
7. Take three from your pile, and then say, "I've got as many cards as you. 3 more, and enough to make your number 14."
8. Ask Jack to show his cards.
9. Let us say Jack has 10 cards.
10. Deal out 10 of your own cards.
11. Next, deal out three of your cards, and then enough cards to bring the total up to 14.
12. You and Jack will have exactly the same number of cards.

Cutting to the Aces

How You Do It:

1. Start by making sure all four Aces are at the top.
2. With your right hand, hold your thumb under the top two Aces.
3. With your thumb still in place, put the deck on the table facedown.
4. With your right hand, cut the deck halfway up.
5. Put the top half 2 or 3 inches away from the bottom.
6. When you bring back your right hand, put those first two Aces on top of the first half of the deck.
7. With both hands, cut both piles in half again, and put the new cuts on the left and right of the first cuts, so that you have four stacks in the shape of a diamond.
8. Take the top cards of the right and left stacks then turn them over. Move them to the top and bottom stacks.

Hint: You are not actually cutting to the Aces, but you are making your audience believe you are!

False Freedom

How You Do It:

1. First, get Jack to shuffle the deck for you.
2. If he does not do a **riffle shuffle**, give the deck to another person to riffle shuffle (do not tell them to do it that way). We will call her Queenie.
3. After the deck has been riffle shuffled, ask Queenie to cut the deck once.
4. Ask, "You could have cut to any card, is that right?"
5. As you ask that question, secretly put a **pinky break** between the top two cards.
6. When Queenie says "yes," lift both cards between your thumb and first two fingers, just as if they were one card.
7. When you lift the cards, show the face of the bottom one to the audience so that you cannot see it.
8. Ask Queenie to memorize the card.
9. Place both cards face-down on table, so they look like one card.
10. Push the top card off the deck so that its face-down in your open hand.
11. Tell Queenie to put her card back into the deck face-down, anywhere she wants.

Now You Know It!

The Riffle Shuffle: In a riffle shuffle, the dealer starts with the deck split in half. One half is put in each hand. The edges are brought close together, and the cards are allowed to fall so that they weave together.

The Pinky Break: The Pinky Break is a sleight-of-hand move in which the dealer inserts their pinky between two

12. Hand Queenie her "card." Her actual card will be on top of the deck, but she will not know that.
13. When she puts the card into the deck, say, "Do you feel like you had free choice to put your card anywhere in the deck?"
14. After she says yes, hand her the deck.
15. Say, "To make sure neither of us know where your card is, can you shuffle the deck again?"
16. As she shuffles, keep your eye on the original card packet (the one with her card on top).
17. If she has left her card on the top after riffling the deck, you do not need to do anything. Jump right to step 27.
18. If the card has moved from the top, stop Queenie before she pushes the two woven packets together.
19. Take the woven cards and fan them out in your hand...make sure you keep them woven together.
20. Tell Queenie her card could be anywhere.
21. As you say that, secretly grab the correct card, along with a few behind it, with your empty hand.
22. Pull them out of the shuffle. It should look like you moved some cards from the deck to your other hand, as if shuffling the deck a bit.
23. Put your hands loosely together, putting these cards on top of the woven cards.
24. Grab more cards from both halves of the shuffle and put them in your free hand.
25. Place them on top of the deck and grab more.
26. This lets you secretly move the chosen card to the top of the deck.
27. Show the cards in the shuffle, and then bring the deck together.
28. Smile and say, "You really shuffled these! If this works, it will really be magic!"
29. Ask Queenie to cut roughly half of the deck into your hand.
30. Set aside the rest of the deck.
31. Ask, "Do you agree that your card may or may not be in with these cards?" (Point to the cards in your hand)

32. When she agrees, say something like, "If I were to tell you that your card was with the cards that you cut, would you be impressed? Probably not. How about this: let's see how many cards you cut off and then I'll see what I can do."

33. As you are talking, secretly put a **pinky break** beneath the top card so that you can look at it. This is the chosen card, so make sure you remember what it is.

34. Grab the packet of cards from above, so that your forefinger is on the top short side and your thumb is on the bottom short side of it.

35. Deal them into your hand. Tell Queenie to count the cards as you do this.

36. While she is counting, spell out the chosen card in your mind. So, if she chooses the Two of Spades, you would think of it like this: T-W-O O-F S-P-A-D-E-S, with each letter being said with each number.

37. Once you have spelled out the card, use the pinky of your deck hand to keep a **pinky break** between the pile already in your hand and any cards that you will deal into your hand from that point.

38. Deal the card like nothing has happened, until they are all in your hand.

39. Let's pretend Queenie counted 36 cards. Announce the number, and then say something like, "Suppose your card is one of those. That is not impressive, right? Would you be impressed if I told you I knew exactly where your card was in the deck?"

40. Add something like, "Would you be more impressed if your card was exactly where I telepathically influenced you to put it?"

41. When she says "yes," ask her to deal the cards onto the table, one at a time, face-down, and speaking a letter aloud for each card.

42. You will need to show Queenie what you mean, so use the Two of Spades, and deal until you get to your pinky break. Make sure you include the "O-F."

43. Say, "and so on," or something like that, to make it look like you were just showing her what to do.
44. If the Two of Spades example is not long enough, just do a **pass** at the **pinky break.**
45. If you do not want to show her what to do using the cards, you can pretend to do it, but still do a **pass** at the right spot.
46. The card above the **pinky break** should now be at the top of the packet. The example cards that you spelled out will be on the table.
47. Take the example cards and put them under the cards you are holding.
48. Hand the packet to Queenie, asking what her card was.
49. When she says what it is, tell her to start spelling the cards onto the table as you showed.
50. When she deals the last card, remind her that she cut and shuffled the deck a number of times during the trick, and that she admitted her card could be anywhere in the deck.
51. Tell Queenie to turn over the last card. It will be her card!

Now You See It!

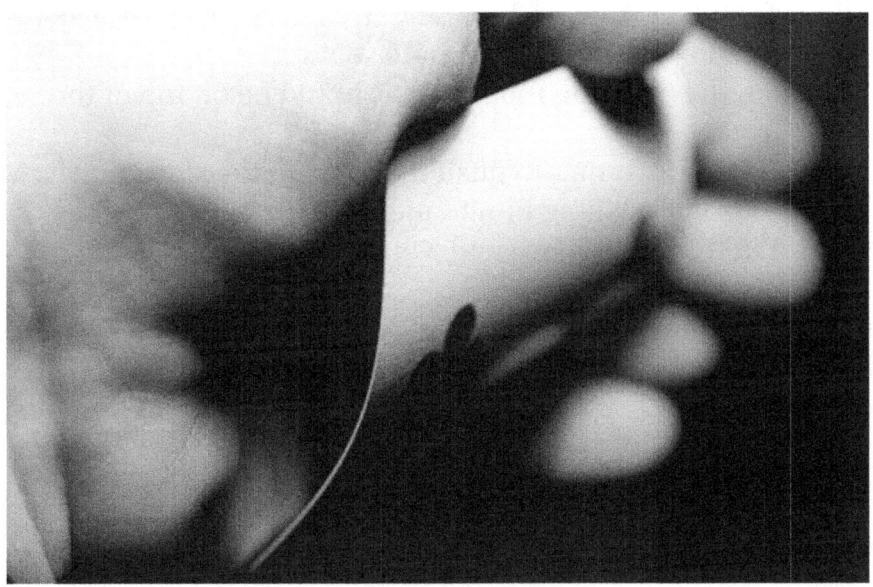

Prepare:

    1.   Get a look at the bottom card and remember it.

How You Do It:

    1.   Do an **overhand shuffle**, but make sure you put the last cards at the top one at a time so that the card on the bottom ends up on top.

    2.   Put both hands behind your back, saying that you want to be as fair as possible when performing the trick.

    3.   While your hands are out of sight, **palm** the top card.

    4.   Turn away from Jack.

    5.   Turn your deck hand so that your palm is facing down, and then put the hand with the card over the back of your deck hand to hide it.

    6.   Ask Jack to the take the deck and shuffle it.

    7.   Keep your hands together to hide the palmed card.

8. When they are done, get him to put the deck back in your hand (you still have your back to him).
9. Next, get Jack to cut any amount of cards from the deck and hold them in his hand.
10. Turn back toward him, secretly putting the palmed card on top of the deck as you do so.
11. So, the card you memorized should be on top of the deck.
12. Use your thumb to push this card to the side and show it to Jack, asking him to memorize the card.
13. Put it back in place and ask Jack to put the packet he cut off back on top.
14. Turning your back toward Jack, hold the pack where he can see it.
15. Ask Jack to shuffle the deck again so that you lose the card.
16. Once he has given you back the deck, turn back toward Him.
17. Spread the cards out so that only you can see them.
18. Pull out a card that is different in color and number.
19. Put it face-down in front of you.
20. Pull out two more cards that are different in color and number and put them on the first card.
21. Find Jack's card (which is the one you first memorized), and put it face-down on top of the other three.
22. Put the deck aside.
23. Using a **glide**, pick up the four cards.
24. Showing Jack the bottom card, ask if it is his.
25. He will say "no." When he does, turn your hand down and perform another **glide.**
26. Put his card face-down near the card you just showed, but a little closer to you.
27. Put the card from the bottom of the packet on the top.
28. Turn the last card in your hand face-up.
29. Ask the Jack if it is his card.
30. Before he can say "no," put it face-down next to the last card, but closer to you.

31. Jack probably will not notice that you showed him the last card twice, since he is only thinking about his own card.

32. Four cards should be face-down in a line on the table. The line of cards should start near Jack and end near you. His card should be the second one from their end of the line.

33. Ask Jack to point to a card, any one.

34. If he points to the second card at their end of the line, turn it over.

35. If he does not, ask him to point to another card. If he picks another that is not his card, pick up both and discard them.

36. There should now be two cards on the table. One of them will be Jack's card.

37. Ask him to turn over the card.

38. Take a bow!

39.

Now You Know It!

Overhand Shuffle: Grab the deck from beneath it, by the top and bottom edges, using your thumb and forefinger. Take some cards in your left hand and bring them to the left. Move your left hand back to the right, grab another bunch of cards, and keep repeating until you're finished the deck.

Palm: The palm move lets the magician hide a certain card in the palm of their hand. It's done by first covering the deck with your hand and putting your thumb near the inner left corner. Use your thumb to guide the card into your hand.

Glide: A Glide is a type of sleight-of-hand move. The magician appears to be pulling out the bottom card, but they are really pulling out the second card from the bottom.

Say Stop

How You Do It:

1. Shuffle and fan out the deck, then let Queenie choose a card.
2. Cut the deck where she took the card.
3. Ask her to put her card on top of the bottom part of the deck.
4. Put the top part of the deck back onto the bottom, putting a <u>pinky break</u> above her card.
5. **Control** the card to the top and do a **false top riffle shuffle**. Keep the card on top.
6. Put Queenie's card on the table with its face down.
7. Get the next card on the top and put it to the left of her card with its face down, and the next top card to the left of that one.
8. Say, "Let's do one more."
9. Deal the next card, face-down, to the right of her card.
10. Now you have four cards on the table. Queenie's card should be the third from the left.
11. Hold her hand, and guide it over the cards, asking her to tell you when to stop.
12. Move Queenie's hand back and forth slowly, going over each card, until she says, "stop."
13. Next, tap her finger on the chosen card, and make sure it is really the card she wanted.
14. If she chose the third card from the left, you can just turn over the card. It will be right.
15. If she did not stop on that card, then gather up the rest of the cards and put them back one card at a time onto the top of the deck.
16. Make sure the chosen card goes onto the deck last to make sure it stays at the top.
17. Put a <u>pinky break</u> under the top card.
18. Say, "You could have chosen any card, but you chose this one. Let me show you something cool."

19. While you are talking, pick up the card and put it back on top.
20. Next, turn the top two over as one, revealing the chosen card to Queenie.
21. Drop her card face-up on the table.

Now You Know It!

Control: Controlling a card simply means to guide it to where you want it top be in the deck.

False Top Riffle Shuffle: This is a move that allows you to fool the audience into thinking the deck was shuffled properly. Instead, you make sure the top card stays on top by letting it fall last.

Find the Card the Hard Way

How You Do It:

1. For this trick, you will need four audience members, with all five of you sitting around a table.
2. Start with the person on your left side. Deal five hands with five cards each, going clockwise.
3. Ask your audience to look at their hands. Let them mentally choose and remember a card from their hand before placing the hand down on the table.
4. Pick up all the hands, starting from the one on your left side. Go clockwise and pick up all the other hands. The last one you pick up should be your hand.
5. Place each of the hands on top of your pile as you are picking them up.
6. In exactly the same way as earlier, deal the cards again.
7. This time, when you pick the hands up, fan each hand out in front of you so your audience can see the faces of the cards.
8. Each time you fan out a hand, ask if anyone can see his or her card.

9. If they do, ask them to point to it.
10. Without looking at the cards, place the fanned-out hand on the table, pull their card out and place it faced down in front them.
11. There may be more than one chosen card in a hand, or there may be none. Either way, it is all right.
12. When everybody has a card, flip them over one by one, asking each person if it is the card they chose.
13. To everybody's amazement, you will get all four right!

Firehouse Jacks

How You Do It:

1. Take four Jacks out of the deck, as well as four random cards.
2. Fan the four Jacks out so that your audience can see them, with the four other cards behind them so the audience cannot see those.
3. Say, "These are the 4 Jack firemen and they were sent to this burning house to put out the fire."
4. Collect the cards together and put them atop the deck.
5. Say, "The first Jack was sent to the bottom floor."
6. Place it in the bottom of the deck. This card will actually be one of the other four cards you chose.
7. Say, "The second Jack was sent to the middle floor."
8. Put it in the deck's middle.
9. Say, "The third Jack was also sent to the middle of the house, because this is where the fire was burning."
10. Put it in the deck's middle.
11. Say, "The last jack was sent to the top of the house."
12. Put it near the deck's top.
13. Then, you can either say, "Every time I knock, one of the Jacks will come out," or you can ask one of your audience members to knock.
14. After each time you knock, flip over the top card on the deck. It will be a Jack.
15. Do these four times to get all the firemen Jacks out of the burning building.

Packet Slap

How You Do It:

1. Get ten cards from the top of the deck. Put them on the table face down.
2. Spread the rest of the cards out for Queenie.
3. Ask her to pick one and memorize it.
4. Let her put their card back where she took it from.
5. Put a **pinky break** above her card as you put the deck back together.
6. **Control** the card to the bottom of the deck, using a **pass**.
7. Palm her card into your hand using your favorite method.

> ## Now You Know It!
>
> ### *False Bottom Riffle Shuffle:*
> Like the Top version, this is a way of making it look like you are shuffling the deck, while keeping the chosen card on the bottom.

8. Give Queenie the deck with your other hand, while you drop the hand hiding her card down to your side.
9. Have Queenie shuffle the deck.
10. Pick up the pile of ten cards with your empty hand.
11. Square the packet with both hands, putting the chosen card at the bottom of the pile.
12. When Queenie is done, have her put the deck to the side.
13. Do a **false bottom riffle shuffle** on the pile.
14. Ask Queenie to hold out her hand and touch her index finger and thumb together.
15. With your own hands, turn her hand palm downward.
16. Put the pile between her fingertips so that she is pinching the cards together along the short end, telling her to keep a good grip.
17. Slap the cards.
18. If there is more than one card left, keep slapping until there is only one left.
19. Have Queenie turn it over. This should be the chosen card.

Jumping Gemini

Prepare:

1. Make sure these cards, in this order, are at the top of the deck: King of Clubs, King of Diamonds, Ten of Spades and Two of Hearts.

How You Do It:

1. Deal the first three cards onto the table, face-down.
2. Pull the Two of Hearts, showing it to the audience before putting it face-down under the other cards.
3. Put down the deck and pick up the four cards.
4. Do an **Elmsley count**.
5. Bring the Two of Hearts up to the second position in the pile.
6. Announce that there are only four cards.
7. Do a **double turnover** and say, "The Two of Hearts is now on top."
8. Flip the two cards as one, so that they face down.
9. Take the top card from the pile and put it on the bottom.
10. Turn over the new top card and Jack see that it is the Two of Hearts before you flip it back over again.
11. Spread out the pile and put the Two of Hearts in the third-from-top position.
12. Gather up the packet and do a **triple turnover**.
13. Turn the three cards over together so they all face down.
14. Put the top card on the table.
15. Do another **double turnover**, saying, "The Two of Hearts is now on top."
16. Turn the two cards over as one.
17. Move the top card to the bottom and turn over the new top card.
18. It will be the Two of Hearts.

19. Push the two top cards to your other hand's fingers, as one, and move them to the bottom of the pile.
20. Make it look like you moved only one card to the bottom.
21. Do another **double turnover** to show the Two of Hearts at the top again.
22. Turn the two cards face down again, as before.
23. Put the top card onto the table, above the other card there.
24. Tell Jack that the trick could be done with four duplicate cards.
25. Do another **triple turnover** to show the top card as the Ten of Spades, and then turn them back over together.
26. Using your non-deck hand, do a double lift but make sure the cards stay face down in a **Biddle grip**.
27. Push the top card of the pile into your deck hand.
28. Turn it over on the pile along with the 2 cards in your other hand.
29. To Jack, it will look like the Ten of Spades was the second card in the pile.
30. Turn the Ten of Spades back over the way you turned it face-up, and then put the 2 cards in a **Biddle grip** on top of the Ten of Spades.
31. Push the two cards, individually, into your non-deck hand and hold them in a **Biddle grip**.
32. Use these two cards to turn over the top card, which will be the Ten of Spades.
33. Put the two cards on top of the Ten of Spades, face-down, and move them all to the side.
34. Push the bottom card of the pile, using your deck-hand fingers, toward your other hand.
35. With your thumb and forefinger on your deck hand, pinch the top and bottom of the Ten of Spades.
36. With your other hand, pull the three cards off the Ten of Spades, turning that card face up.

37. Use these three to flip the Ten of Spades back over. Place the three on top of that card and gather up the pile.
38. Do a **Flushtration count**, showing each card to be the Ten of Spades.
39. Do a **Gemini count,** showing Kings in this order: red, black, red, black.
40. Use your thumbs to cover the suit symbols of the Kings, and don't call them out, because you will show two of the same cards twice.

Now You Know It!

Elmsley Count: This is a sleight-of-hand move that makes it look like the card is jumping from one pile to another.

Double Turnover: This is a sleight-of-hand move in which you lift 2 cards as one.

Triple Turnover: As with the double version, but with 3 cards.

Biddle Grip: The Biddle Grip lets you to transfer one break to another. Hold the deck between the thumb and middle finger. Put your ring finger next to your middle

Impossible Catch

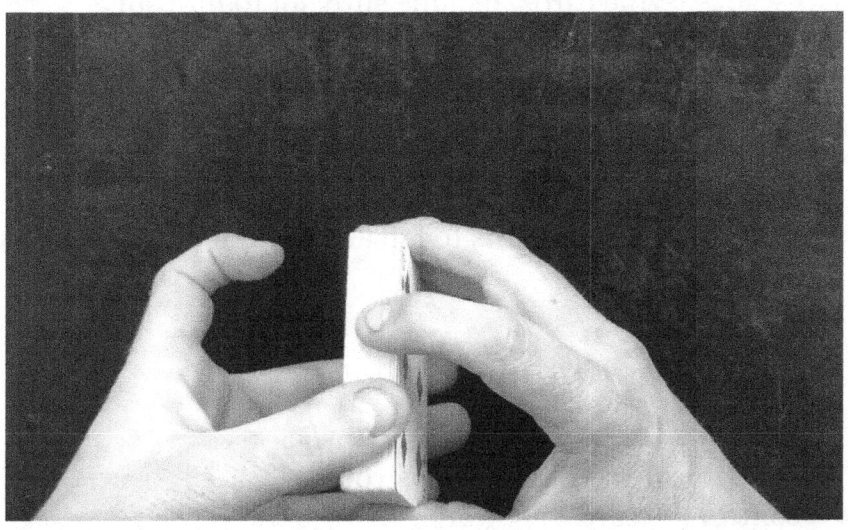

How You Do It:

1. Have Queenie pick a card.
2. Cut the deck where she took her card from.
3. Give Queenie a pen or a permanent marker so she can sign her card.
4. When she puts her card back onto the bottom part of the deck, pull the card out a little bit before putting the top half of the deck on it, so that you can keep track of where it is.
5. Use a finger to push the card up a bit and put a break under it.
6. With a **Bottom Herrmann Pass**, guide the card to the bottom.
7. Do a few **bottom retention overhand shuffles**, making sure to keep the signed card on the bottom.
8. <u>Palm</u> the bottom card.
9. Lower your non-deck hand while using your other hand to lift the deck.

10. Hold the deck so that it is in front of you, with the bottom card facing Queenie.
11. **Spring** the cards, making sure not to hit your audience.
12. Quickly shoot the hand with the palmed card into the falling cards.
13. Use your pinky finger to flick that card up to your fingertips so that it looks like you caught it in mid-air.
14. Wait for all the cards to fall and your audience to react.

Now You Know It!

Bottom Herrmann Pass: This is a sleight-of-hand that allows you to control the card to bottom.

Bottom Retention Overhand Shuffle: This is a false shuffle that allows you to keep the bottom pile on the bottom.

Spring: This is when you bend the deck away from you and let the cards shoot outward.

Four Ace Extravaganza

Prepare:

1. Take all the aces out of the deck, along with the 2, 3, 4, 5, 6, 7, 8, and 9 cards in all the suits.
2. Put the 4 Aces at the top.
3. Put the numbered cards in order from 2 to 9 and then put them on top of the Aces.
4. The top of the deck should be in this order: 2, 3, 4, 5, 6, 7, 8, 9, A, A, A, A.
5. The rest of the deck can be put below that bunch of cards.

How You Do It:

1. Make a bet with Jack. Tell him that you will be able to locate all the aces.
2. Shuffle the deck. However, ensure that the twelve cards on the top stay there.
3. Ask Jack to give you a number between 10 and 19, then put that many cards on the table face-down.
4. Have Jack add together the two digits in his number and give you the total.
5. Take the pile off the table and put that many cards back on the deck.
6. Take the top card from the pile and put it face-up on the table. It should be the first Ace.
7. Put the rest of the cards from the pile on the top of the deck without changing their order.
8. Shuffle without changing the order of the top 11 cards.
9. Repeat steps 3-6 two more times.
10. Put the deck in front of Jack, face-down.
11. Ask him to give you a number between 1 and 9.
12. Have them count that number of cards onto the table, face-down, and turn the last card face-up.
13. If their number was 9, they will turn over an Ace.

14. If their number was something different, they will turn up either a 9, 8, 7, 6, 5, 4, 3 or 2.
15. Ask Jack to deal out the same number of cards as the value of the card they turned over. The card that has been turned over counts as the first one.
16. The fourth Ace will be the last card.

Jack Attack

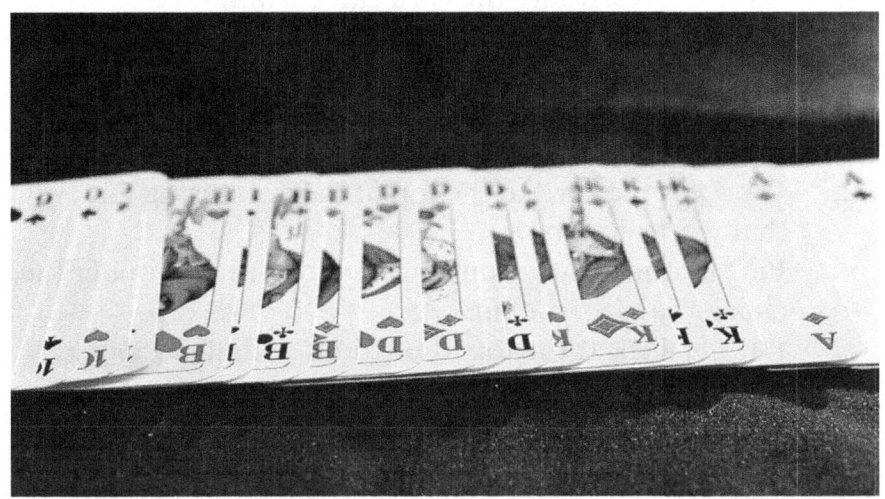

Prepare:

1. Take out the Jack of Clubs and the Jack of Spades.
2. Place one of the jacks at the top of the deck. Place the other one at the bottom.

How You Do It:

1. Do a **bottom retention overhand shuffle,** but pull out only the top and bottom cards for the first part of the shuffle.
2. Do another **bottom retention overhand shuffle**, but this time complete the shuffle.
3. When you get to the last card, put it on top of the deck. This will leave you with one Jack on the top and one on the bottom.
4. With your thumb and forefinger, pinch the deck together on the bottom.
5. Throw the deck into your free hand, but make sure you keep the top and bottom cards.
6. Turn these 2 cards face-up, and say, "I'll need these for the trick."
7. Put the Jacks on the table face-up.

8. Spread the deck. Let Queenie pick a card and memorize it.
9. Cut the deck where the card came from.
10. Ask Queenie to put her card on top of the bottom half of the deck.
11. Stick a **pinky break** above the card when you put the top of the deck on.
12. **Control** the card to the top of the deck using any way that works for you.
13. Pick up the 2 Jacks, putting a **pinky break** under the chosen card as you do.
14. Put the Jack at the top of the deck with its face up.
15. Lift the 3 cards (the chosen card and the 2 Jacks) using a Biddle grip.
16. Put the top card from the pile of 3 on top of the deck, face-up.
17. You should have a Jack on the deck and one in your hand, with the chosen card hidden under it.
18. Put the 2 cards you are holding face-up on the other Jack, only covering half of it.
19. Pull the 2 cards out a tiny bit, so you don't lose track of them.
20. Slide the 2 cards forward, leaving only the top Jack in sight.
21. Slide the top Jack backward, leaving the chosen card and making it look as though the bottom Jack is gone.
22. Say, "The first Jack is looking for your card."
23. Do a **Herrmann pass**, wave your hand, and make the second Jack disappear.
24. Say, "Now both Jacks are looking for your card."
25. Spread out the cards until you get to the two Jacks (which are face-up).
26. The chosen card will be between them. Have Queenie turn over her card.

Magic Magnets Color Separation

Prepare:

1.   Divide the deck into reds and blacks.

How You Do It:

1.   So that it looks like you are mixing the cards, have one of your audience members deal the deck into 4 face-down piles.

2.   Riffle any 2 piles together, and then repeat for the two other piles.

3.   Next, riffle shuffle the remaining two piles together.

4.   Cut the top 1/3 of your deck and put it face-down to your left.

5.   Cut the bottom 1/3 of your deck and put it face-down on your right.

6.   Next, spread the center pile out, face-up, and say that you are going to take out two color magnets.

7.   In reality, you will make sure that the deck is separated into red and black.

8.   Take any 2 cards from the deck, 1 black and 1 red.

9.   Tell your audience that these cards will be your color magnets.

10.   Make a note of which color is at the bottom of the pile; let's pretend its black.

11.   If a black card is at the bottom of the pile, that means that the pile to your left is red and the pile to your right is black.

12.   Collect up your middle pile, and put it face-down.

13.   Now you have three piles. The black ones are on the right, whereas the red ones are on the left.

14.   Take the black color magnet and put it on the top of the right pile. Conversely, put the red color magnet on the top of the left pile.

15.   Time to show the audience! Do a finger snap then show them that the black magnet has attracted all of the

black cards and the red magnet has attracted all the red cards.

16. Next, get the black color magnet. Put it at the bottom of the center pile.
17. Take the red magnet and place it atop the center pile.
18. Do a finger snap again and fan out the center pile face-up, showing that it has been separated into red and black.
19. Take a bow!

Mystical 8s Prediction

Prepare:

1. Start by taking the 4 eights out of the deck.
2. Put the first one on top of the deck.
3. Count 7 cards from the bottom of the deck and put the second card in the eighth space.
4. Put the third card in the ninth space from the bottom.
5. Count to 9 cards, starting from the top of the deck. Slip the 4th card into the tenth space.

How You Do It:

1. Do a false shuffle to make it look like you are mixing the deck. It only needs to look like you are shuffling the deck. The eights need to stay in the same position.
2. Tell your audience you are going to make a random prediction.
3. Take the tenth card from the top of the deck, and put it face-down in front of you, saying that it will be your prediction card.
4. Next, turn the deck face-up, and start dealing cards into one pile.

5. Tell your audience to say stop whenever they like. While you are saying this, make sure you pass your next two eights, so that the trick doesn't get mixed up.
6. When the audience says stop, remember what pile the two eights are in, and flip the dealt pile face-down.
7. This is your first pile.
8. Flip the rest of the pack face-down beside it.
9. This is your second pile.
10. Tell the audience to choose a pile.

If they choose the pile with the eights in the eighth and ninth positions:

1. Tell them you will count out some cards from that pile.
2. Then, take the top card of the other pile and turn it over. This card should be an eight.
3. Count out the next eight cards and put them face-down.
4. Put the rest of the pile you counted from next to it.
5. Turn over the top two cards on that pile.
6. They will be eights like you predicted!

If they choose the pile with the eight on top:

1. Turn over the top card, which will be an eight.
2. Count out eight more cards into a pile face-down.
3. Put the counted pile face-down beside the eight.
4. Turn over the top two cards.
5. These will be the two 8s. You will now have three eights showing. When you turn over your prediction, you will have all four eights!

Paper and Predictions

How You Do It:

1. Let one of your audience members shuffle the deck.
2. Take the deck and secretly get a look at the bottom card.
3. Take the cards and lay them on the table. Say that you have a prediction about a card the will appear later.
4. On a piece of paper, write down the card you saw at the bottom of the deck.
5. Fold the paper so your audience can't see what you wrote.
6. Give the paper to one of your audience members and tell them not to open it.
7. Ask someone to cut the deck and give the top half to the person with the paper.
8. Ask the person with the paper to shuffle their half of the deck to choose any card from it and then lay that card on the table with its face up.
9. Look at the card and count how many symbols are on it. For example, the Six of Diamonds will have a total of 8 diamond symbols on it.
10. Count off that number of cards from your half of the deck, face-up, but stop before you turn over the last card.
11. Tell the person with the paper to read what you wrote and show your prediction to everyone else.
12. When they are doing this, switch the top card on your deck with the bottom card. Make sure they don't notice.
13. When they look back towards you, take the new top card, flip it, and lay it down on the table. This card will be the one that at the beginning you had expected.

Aces Memory

Prepare:

1. Make sure that there is an Ace, a King, and a Queen in that exact order at the bottom of the deck. The suit does not matter.

How You Do It:

1. Show Jack the trio of cards at the deck's bottom. Tilt the deck so he's unable to see the bottom anymore.
2. Explain that the Ace, the King, and the Queen will be taken from the bottom, in that specific order. Pretend to pull out the Ace using your middle finger.
3. In reality, you will be sliding the card toward you using your left ring finger. At the same time, your right middle finger slides out the King. Put the King on the tabletop.
4. Take the subsequent card out of the deck by sliding it out. Jack will think that this is the King. However, this

will be the Ace. Put it down on the right side of the King.

5. Pull the Queen out and put it down on the right side of the others.

6. Jack will think the order of the cards on the table is Ace-King-Queen. In reality, it is actually King-Ace-Queen.

7. Pick up the Ace (middle card) and put it on top of the first card on the left, and then put both cards on top of the third one.

8. Pick up the cards without letting Jack see them.

9. Deal out the 3 cards in a row, left to right.

10. Repeat step 7

11. Pretend to deal them out like before, but secretly deal out from the bottom instead.

12. Ask Jack to tell you where the Ace is.

13. If your trick fooled him, he will think the Ace is the card on the left.

14. If it didn't, he will think it is in the middle.

15. Actually, the Ace will be the card on the right, so Jack will be wrong either way.

Any Way You Count Them

How You Do It:

1. Shuffle the deck completely.
2. Hold it face-down with your hand. Turn the top card over onto the tabletop
3. Starting with that card's value, count cards onto that pile (face-up) until you reach 10. So, if your card is a 3, deal 7 cards onto the pile.
4. Face cards can be thought of as 10, so if you have a face card, you don't need to count anymore.
5. Keep making piles the same way, until you have dealt out the entire deck.
6. If you don't have enough cards to make the last pile, keep that pile in your hand.
7. Pick any 3 piles, as long as they have at least 4 cards in each.
8. Turn these piles face-down.
9. Gather together the rest of the cards and add them to the ones you are holding.
10. Pick two of the three piles that are faced down.
11. Turn over the top card on each of them.
12. Get the sum of their values (remembering that face cards=10).
13. Count out that number of cards from the pile in your hand and discard them.
14. Next, discard 19 more cards.
15. Count the cards left in your hand.
16. Turn the top card on the third pile over. The value of this card will be equal to the number of cards you are holding.

Eight Threatening Kings

Prepare:

1. You need to stack the deck.
2. The order should be eight, King, three, ten, two, seven, nine, five, Queen, four, Ace, six, Jack. It's a good idea to come up with a way to remember the order.
3. The order of the suits should be **CHaSeD** (Clubs, Hearts, Spades, Diamonds).
4. Your deck should have these two patterns over and over until it is completely stacked.

How You Do It:

1. Hold the deck and have Queenie choose and pull out a card.
2. As she looks at the card, start cutting the deck where she pulled the card from and put the top pile on the bottom.
3. Make sure you sneak in a look at the card on the bottom.

4. Think of the word from the rhyme that matches the card's value.

5. For example, if the card is a four of hearts, the word you want is "For."

6. The next word in the rhyme is "One," which is meant to be the Ace.

7. Next, figure out the card's suit letter from CHaSeD. If the card were the Four of Hearts, the letter would be H. The letter after H is S (Spades).

8. Using that method of figuring, tell Queenie what her card is (Ace of Spades, in my example).

Now You Know It!

A good way to remember the order in the Eight Threatening Kings Trick is to use this rhyme: "Eight Kings Threatened to Save Ninety-Five Queens For One Sick Knave."

Get Money

How You Do It:

1. Take the Jokers out, and then shuffle your deck.
2. Fan out the cards on the table, face-down, and ask Jack to pick one.
3. Have him show the card to others, but not you.
4. Shuffle again, cut close to the middle, and let him put his card back.
5. Try to look at the card (the Key Card) that will be on top of his, but don't let Jack see you look.
6. Make a single cut, but you can do it as many times as you like.
7. When you are finished cutting the deck, sneak in a look at the bottommost card.
8. If the bottommost card happens to be the Key Card, cut the cards again.
9. Place the deck face down on the table.
10. Start flipping over the cards, and keep going until you get to the one after the Key Card.
11. This will be the audience's chosen card, so remember it.
12. Hold the next card in the deck as if you are about to flip it over.
13. Say, "I'll bet you all one dollar each that the next card I turn over will be yours."
14. Once they take the bet, flip over their card and collect your reward.

Math Magic

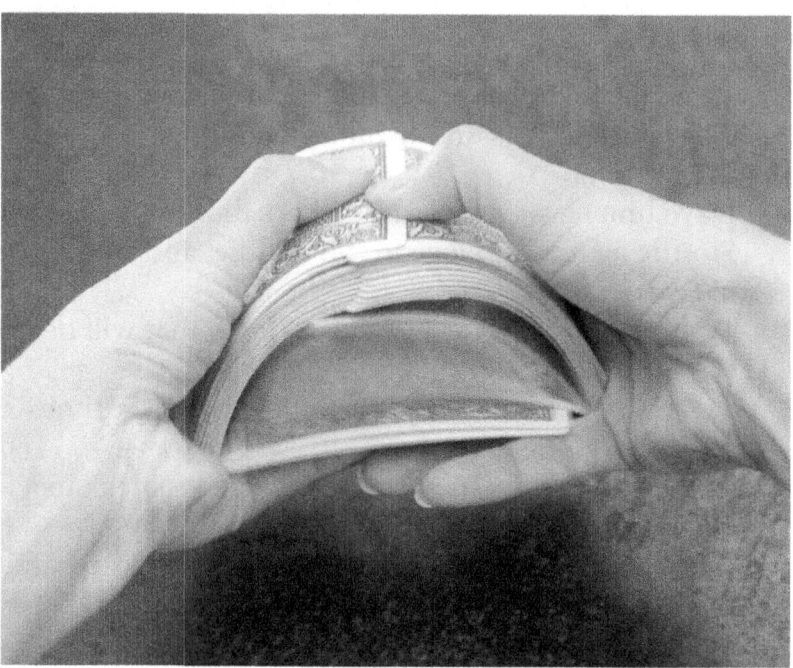

How You Do It:

1. Deal 3 cards, face-up, in a row going from the left to the right.
2. Below that, overlapping the first row, deal out 3 more cards. Their faces should be visible.
3. Keep dealing like that until you have 3 columns with 7 cards each.
4. Ask Jack to choose a card in their mind and tell you which column it is in (not which card).
5. Gather the columns, one at a time. Do not change their order. Take them all in your hand. The pile that contains the chosen card should be in the middle between the other two piles.
6. Deal the cards once again into 3 columns of 7 cards.
7. Ask your audience member which column their card is in.
8. Gather up the cards the same way you did in step 5.

9. Repeat steps 6-8.
10. The chosen card should now be the 11th card from the top.
11. Take 3 cards from the pack, as one group, and put them face-down on the tabletop.
12. Take another group of three to the right of that pile, and then another group to the right of that too.
13. Below the three groups, create another group with 3 piles of 3 cards each.
14. Place the final group of three cards below the column in the middle.
15. Ask the audience member to touch any of the three piles.
16. If they touch the pile at the far left of the second row (we'll call it PFLSHC), then you would pick up the other 4 piles.
17. Set them aside.
18. If they don't touch PFLSHC, then you would pick up the 3 piles they did touch and set them aside.
19. Move the other piles around but remember where you put PFLSHC.
20. Ask the audience member to touch 2 random piles.
21. Take away the piles as you did in steps 16 or 18, but don't remove PFLSHC.
22. Keep removing piles this way, until you only have PFLSHC left.
23. Next, spread out the 3 cards in that pile and have the audience member choose 2 cards.
24. Take away the cards that are picked, but don't remove the middle card.
25. Turn it over.
26. It will be the card the audience member chose.

No, I Got It!

How You Do It:

1. Hold your deck in your hand.
2. Make three piles of cards. Keep at least 20 cards in your hand. The amount of cards in each pile does not matter.
3. Tell Jack to pick a card from the top of one of the 3 piles, and then put it back once he's looked at it.
4. While Jack is distracted, palm a random card into your hand.
5. When his card is back in place, put your hand atop the same pile. Say, "Would you like me to hit the cards like this?"
6. While your hand is on top of the pile, secretly put the palmed card on top of their card.
7. Next, touch the pile with your finger and say "Or would you like me to hit the cards like this?"
8. Whichever way they choose, hit all 3 piles the same way.
9. Tell them you are going to move their card to another pile.
10. Pick up the card that you put on top of their card and move it to another pile.
11. Pick up the other 2 piles, with the pile containing their card on top.
12. Ask your audience if they kept an eye on the card. They will probably say "yes."
13. If they said yes, ask them to turn over the card they think is the right one.
14. When they turn over the wrong card, say, "Nope! I've got it!"
15. Show them the right card.

The Story of Cactus Pete

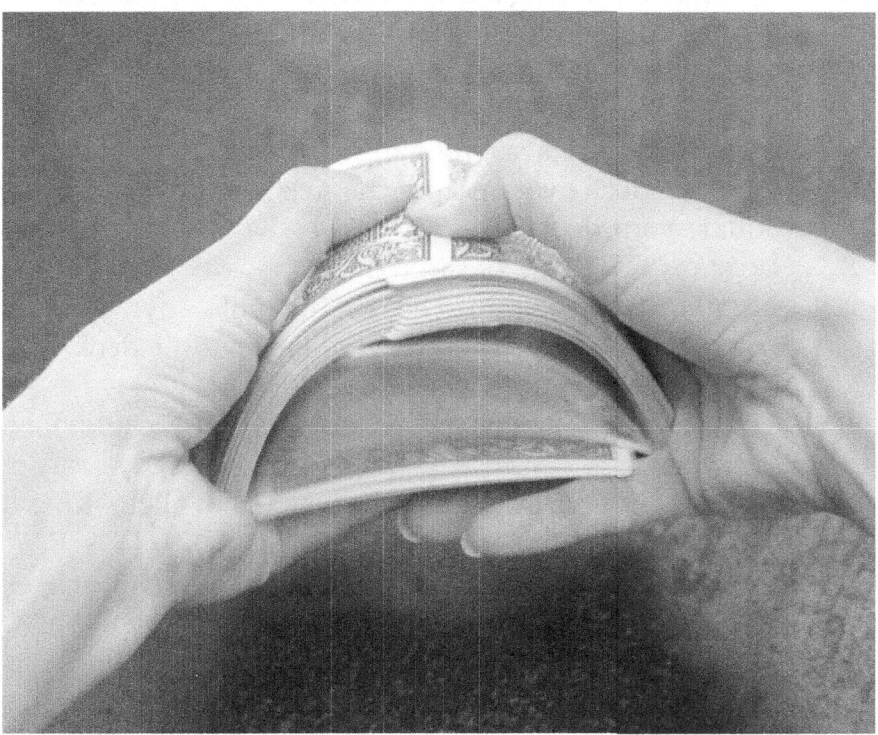

Prepare:

1. This trick needs a stacked deck.
2. From the bottom card, the order of the cards should be random card, Ace, King, Ace, King, Ace, King, King. It doesn't matter what the suits are.
3. There will be two sleights: a **false cut** and a **glide.**

How You Do It:

1. Bring out your deck of cards and say to your audience that you are going to tell them the story of Cactus Pete, the King of the Card Sharps.

2. Say, "You see, no matter where Cactus Pete cut, he would always cut to an Ace."
3. Cut the deck, using a **false cut**. That gets the random card out of the way, without the audience knowing it.
4. When you pull the Ace out, do a <u>glide</u> and take the King behind the Ace out at the same time.
5. Show that you have cut to an Ace, just like Cactus Pete.
6. Turn the deck over and put the Ace face-down.
7. Square your deck.
8. Do steps 1-7 a total of three times.
9. After you place the third ace on the table, say, "Because, you see, no matter where Cactus Pete cut the deck, he would always cut to a what?"
10. Cut the deck again, as before, but wait for the audience to say "Ace."
11. Say, "Nope, a King, because he was Cactus Pete, King of the Card Sharps!"
12. Turn over the last card you cut to and reveal a King.
13. Turn over the three "Aces" you cut to and reveal that they are Kings!

Think About It

Prepare!

1. Make 4 piles, one for each suit.
2. Arrange the pile in order from the King on top to the Ace at the bottom.
3. Face the piles up. Arrange them so that they are arranged as such (L to R): spades, hearts, clubs, and diamonds.
4. Cut the Spades pile so that the King is turned up with the Ace underneath.
5. Cut the Hearts pile so that the 4 is turned up.
6. Cut the Clubs pile so that the 7 is turned up.
7. Cut the Diamond pile so that the 4 is turned up.
8. In this specific order, place these four cards in a pile facing down: King of Spades, Ten of Hearts, Seven of Clubs, and Four of Diamonds.
9. Put the rest of the deck underneath those four cards, in the order of suits (Spades, Hearts, Clubs, Diamonds)
10. The deck is now ready.

How You Do It:

1. Cut the deck in half several times, so that it looks like you are shuffling the deck. Don't change the order of the cards, though.
2. Hold the deck out in front of you.
3. Ask someone to cut it, putting the top part of the cut next to the bottom part, and then take the top card off the left pile.
4. Place the right pile under the left pile.
5. Get a look at the bottom card on the right pile, without anyone knowing.
6. In your head, add 3 to the number on the bottom card. This will tell you what the chosen card is.
7. Let's pretend the bottom card is a nine. That means the chosen card is a Queen. If the bottom card were a

Queen, then the chosen would be a two (start the count over after the King, with Aces being a low card).

8. To figure out the suit, remember **CHaSeD**.
9. If a spade is on the bottom, then the chosen card is a Diamond.
10. If the 6 of Diamonds is on the bottom, that means the chosen card is the 9 of Clubs.
11. If the 10 of Clubs is on the bottom, the King of Hearts is the chosen card.

From Here to There

How You Do It:

1. Fan the cards out. Tell Jack to pick one.
2. Ask him to memorize the card.
3. Fan the cards once more and ask him to put his card back.
4. Watch where Jack puts his card.
5. Cut the deck, making sure that it puts his card on the bottom. If he notices, it's alright.
6. Hold the deck up so that Jack can see his card. Ask him if it's his.
7. When he says "yes," get two cards—one card at a time—and place them at the bottom of the deck under Jack's card.

8. Hold the deck up once more. However, this time, hold it in your right hand with your thumb on the left side of the deck and the other fingers on the right side.

9. Ask Jack again. Jack should say "no," but if he does not, repeat step 7 until he does say "no."

10. Using the same hand position, face the deck down and give Jack the bottommost card.

11. As you do this, curl your pinky and ring fingers downward to push the bottommost card into your palm.

12. Get the second card from the bottom. Jack will think this is his card. Put this card in his hand.

13. Repeat step 7.

14. Jack should have three cards.

15. Set the deck aside and take Jack's three cards.

16. Redo step 11 and step 12 but with the three cards instead of the rest of the deck.

17. Show Jack that the last two cards are not his.

18. Ask him to look at the card in his hand. That will be Jack's card.

Calling the Shots

How You Do It:

1. Without letting Queenie know, sneak a look at the bottom of the deck.
2. Keep the bottom card where it is, using a false shuffle.
3. For this example, let us say that the bottom card was the Four of Clubs.
4. As you are doing your false shuffle, tell Queenie that in a minute, you will need her to pick some cards without seeing what they are.
5. Place the deck down onto the tabletop with its face down.
6. Tell Queenie to take the card on the top of the deck and put it on the tabletop with the face down.
7. For a few minutes, make it look like you are concentrating on that card.
8. The goal is to make Queenie believe you are psychic.
9. Say, "It's the Four of Clubs."
10. Pick up the card and give it a look, but don't let Queenie see the card.
11. Say, "Yup, I'm right."
12. The card you picked up isn't actually the Four of Clubs, or whatever card was at the bottom, but you want Queenie to believe it is for the moment.
13. Before putting the card back down on the table, look at it and memorize it.
14. Let's pretend it's the Three of Hearts.
15. Ask Queenie to pick a random card from the middle of the deck and put it on the table like before.
16. Repeat step 7.
17. Concentrate on the card again and say, "It's the Three of Hearts."
18. Look at the card again and say, "I'm right again!"
19. Like before. don't let Queenie see the card. Put it down.

20. Ask Queenie to pick a card from the bottom and lay it down.
21. Concentrate on the card for a few moments.
22. Say "It's the Queen of Hearts."
23. Pick up the card, look at it without giving Queenie a look, and say, "I'm right."
24. If Queenie is smart, she won't believe you.
25. Ask her what cards you said to pick out of the deck.
26. Take the three cards in front of you and, with a little sleight-of-hand, arrange them so that they are in the order you called them in.
27. Remember, Queenie hasn't seen the cards.
28. As she says, "Top, middle, bottom," or something like that, drop the right card before them.
29. Tell Queenie you hypnotized her so that she would draw those particular cards.

Count on Me

How You Do It:

1. Ask Jack to shuffle a pack of cards that **isn't yours.**
2. When he's done, ask him to deal out any number of cards less than 15 and remember what the last card is.
3. Have him replace the cards in the deck, in the same order he dealt them out in (so that the first card he dealt out goes back last).
4. While Jack is doing all this, you should have your back to him.
5. When he is done, turn around.
6. Hold the deck behind your back.
7. Being careful not to change their order around, count 15 cards from the top and put them on the bottom of the deck.
8. Make it look like you are struggling to keep a hold on the deck and having trouble finding a certain card.
9. When you are done, give Jack back his deck.

10. Have him check that the card he memorized is not within the first (however many he counted) cards of the deck.
11. Tell him to transfer the amount he counted from the top to the bottom.
12. Once this is done, put the deck behind your back and transfer 15 cards from the bottom to the top.
13. After you've counted off and transferred 15 cards, pull out the one that is now on the bottom, and show it to Jack.
14. It will be the card he memorized.

Fool Proof Reversed Card

Prepare:

1. Your deck needs to have 2 cards that are exactly the same.
2. Put one of them in the 9th position of a face-down deck.
3. Put the other one, face-up, in the 21st position of the deck.

How You Do It:

1. Put the deck face-down on the table, all nicely squared.
2. Ask Queenie to choose a number from 10 to 19, and then have her deal that number of cards from the top.
3. Next, ask her to add together the two digits in her number and then deal that number of cards from the pile back onto the deck.
4. Ask Queenie to turn over the next card in the pile. This will be one of the cards you already positioned in the deck.
5. Make sure everyone at the table, including you, can see it.
6. Ask Queenie to put this card on the top of the deck, followed by the cards from the pile.
7. Next, ask Queenie to cut the deck 5 times. Actually, she can cut it as often as she wants, but if she does it only 2-3 times, the card may show up too early.
8. This next part is key, so make it seem really important, and watch carefully to make sure it's done properly.
9. Have Queenie turn the whole deck over in her hands 3 times.
10. Next, ask Queenie to search through the deck for the card.
11. As the trick name says, the card will be reversed.
12. Because you never touch the deck yourself during the trick, Queenie will be amazed that she performed a card trick.

Fifteen Card Trick

Prepare:

Before presenting this outstanding trick take the time to lay three of the playing cards on the edge of a table that you have set up to be near you. 2. Place two standard envelopes on top of three cards, so as to completely hide the three cards from the view of your spectators. Be careful to take the time to ensure that these cards are completely concealed from view as they are ultimately going to be the key to pulling off the entire trick successfully.

How to Do it:

1. For starters, you will need to give the deck (minus the three cards) to a spectator before asking him or her to count out a total of 15 cards. As they do so, ensure that they count aloud and place each of the cards face down on the table as they do so. For an added flourish you can remove yourself from the vicinity while they are counting.

2. Once the 15 cards have been counted out and are laying face down on the table, the next step is to ask the person who counted the cards to either pass the rest of the deck to a second volunteer or to hold onto them very tightly. Regardless, do what you can to make sure you never touch the cards yourself.

3. If you are using two volunteers then you will want to ask the first to place their hands firmly on the table, otherwise ensure they are holding the deck of cards tightly. You will want to exaggerate this part as well in order for the reveal to really work.

4. Next you will want to pick up the envelope that is hiding the three cards, while at the same time palming the cards so that the audience can't see what you are doing. You will then want to appear to casually toss the first envelope onto the pile of cards, positioning the extra cards on top of the rest as you do so. You will then want to casually throw out the second envelope as well.

5. With this done you will want to ask the volunteers to pick up both envelopes and ensure that there aren't any extra

cards inside. Only one envelope is required for the trick but using two sells the illusion even more as it gives the volunteer more choice.

6. Once one or both of the volunteers have looked over the envelopes you will then ask them to "scoop up" the cards and place them in the envelope. This is important phrasing as it will put it in the mind of the volunteer(s) that they are supposed to pick the cards up quickly as opposed to doing it one at a time as they did when they originally chose them.

7. With the cards in the envelope, ask one of the volunteers to seal the envelope and place it in their pocket.

8. If one of the volunteers is still holding the deck, tell them to be sure to hold on tight because you are just about to make three additional cards appear in the sealed envelope.

9. This next part is going to make or break the trick and it is all up to you on how you sell it. You are going to want to make it appear as though you are mentally drawing three additional cards from the deck and shooting them into the envelope. Of all the aspects of the trick this is likely the one you will want to practice the most.

10. With the pantomime completed, you will then ask the volunteer holding the deck to set them down on the table as they are no longer needed. Ask the volunteer with the envelope in their pocket to remove the envelope, break the seal and count the cards.

11. To everyone's surprise, there will now be 18 cards in the envelope as opposed to 15.

Taking it to the next level:
1. For an extra flourish, while the envelope is being opened and the cards counted, you can take the remainder of the deck from the second volunteer as opposed to having them place the deck on the table. When taking the deck you are going to want to palm three of the cards before placing the rest of the deck on the table separate from any other cards.

2. As soon as it is revealed that there are 18 cards instead of the expected 15, smile and say that you believe the volunteer counted incorrectly. As you do so, place one hand

on the shoulder of the first volunteer while causally placing your other hand on the pile of cards, but only for long enough to drop off the remaining cards.

3. After dropping off the cards say, "By the snap of my finger, I can—before your very eyes—add three more cards to that pile (pointing to the 18 cards), then you will have 21 cards."

4. With an additional flourish, you will then snap your fingers, and request someone to count out the cards again, and of course, 21 cards will be in the pile.

5. If you are very quick you will be able to place your hand on the pile after the 21 cards have been counted and palm 3 of them once more. If so, you can then repeat the process above only in reverse so that with another snap of your fingers you can make 3, or even 6, of the cards disappear once more on cue.

Conclusion

Well, there you go.

Cards are great things. They can be a cheap source of fun, whether you are using them to play card games or to fool your friends and family. You can keep them at home or stash them in a bag and take them anywhere. They can be as plain or as fancy as you want. With a little crafty know-how, you could even make a deck of cards yourself!

The wonderful thing about card magic is that the tricks can be simple, or they can be complicated. They can be done for your own amusement, or in front of your friends and family for their entertainment, or they can be performed in front of a bigger audience as the master magicians do.

The tricks included in this eBook are not basic, and they will challenge you. They will make you think, and you will need to practice to be able to do them without a problem.

But hey!

Once upon a time, you thought even basic card tricks were hard to do, and now you can probably do those with one hand behind your back.

Since you have gotten so good at doing basic card tricks, trying out the tricks included in this Book should be no big deal, right?

You have started amazing your friends and family with your card magic skills. Now, with practice, you can really leave them wondering how you did it.

Read through all the tricks, learn something new, but most of all, have some fun!

Best,

Andrew Howell

Made in the USA
Monee, IL
12 February 2021

60347183R00038